PINEAPPLES
AND
PRAISE

BY BETHANY MARSHALL
ILLUSTRATED BY SARAH VOGEL

Illustrated by Sarah Vogel

ISBN: 978-1-7343431-4-4 (Print)
        978-1-7343431-5-1 (E-book)

Printed in the U.S.A.

This book is dedicated
to children and families
around the world.

A PINEAPPLE IS **UNIQUE;**
THAT'S WHAT SOME
MAY THINK.

4

For how it GROWS
is unusual but
also quite neat!

WATCHING A PINEAPPLE GROW IS REALLY A **SIGHT**.

6

THE CROWN IS **PLANTED** AND SITS UP JUST RIGHT.

One by one, a pineapple **AWAITS**.

BUT THE **GROWTH** OF A PINEAPPLE
IS BEAUTIFUL AND GREAT.

10

DEEP WITHIN THE CROWN,
A FLOWER IS IN SIGHT.
LOOK AT THE COLORS;
THEY ARE SO VIBRANT
AND BRIGHT!

WATCH AS THEY **FORM**
FROM A FLOWER TO A FRUIT.
PINEAPPLES ARE
SO COLORFUL AND CUTE!

12

14

WHEN A PINEAPPLE GROWS, WE SEE IT SO **CLEAR**.

THE PINEAPPLE'S **CROWN** RISES,
AND THE FRUIT APPEARS.

Just like a pineapple, **YOU** have a crown, And one day

That crown will be **LAID** on the ground.

18

The crown will be given
to the one who
KNOWS you most,
praising Him
and singing,
all creation
will **BOAST**.

PINEAPPLES AND PRAISE ARE ONE
AND THE SAME; ONE DAY, EVERYTHING
WILL **GLORIFY** HIS NAME!

Like pineapples standing tall and leaves **REACHING** high, we can **SING** praises to our Lord and glorify.

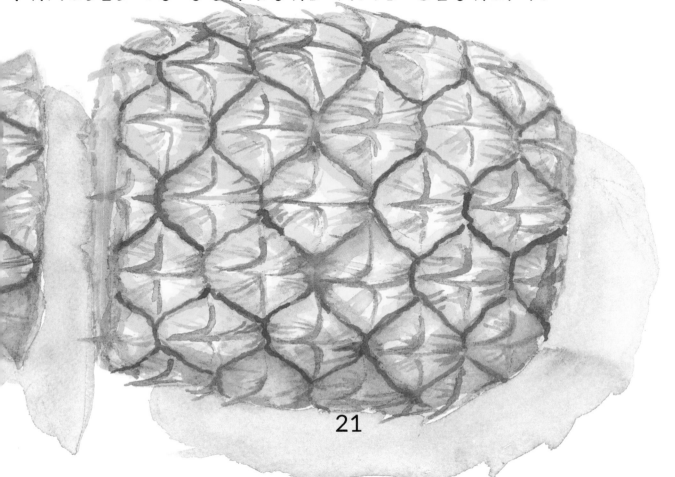

PRAISE IS A SONG
AND **VICTORIOUS** SOUND.
PRAISE COMES FROM PEOPLE
WHO WERE **LOST**
BUT NOW **FOUND**.

23

24

Jesus is King, He is Lord over **ALL**.
So, praise Him! Praise Him!
Big, medium,
or **SMALL**!

PINEAPPLES
HAVE CROWNS,
AND WE HAVE
THEM TOO.

26

SO **GIVE** HIM THE PRAISE
IN ALL THAT YOU **DO**.

Psalm 150

Praise the Lord.
Praise God in his sanctuary;
praise him in his mighty heavens.
Praise him for his acts of power;
praise him for his surpassing greatness.
Praise him with the sounding of the trumpet,

PRAISE HIM WITH THE HARP AND LYRE,
PRAISE HIM WITH TIMBREL AND DANCING,
PRAISE HIM WITH THE STRINGS AND PIPE,
PRAISE HIM WITH THE CLASH OF CYMBALS,
PRAISE HIM WITH RESOUNDING CYMBALS.
LET EVERYTHING THAT HAS BREATH PRAISE THE LORD.
PRAISE THE LORD!

About Bethany Marshall

Bethany Marshall is the family life pastor at Trans4mation Church; she is also the founder and director of Daughters Conference, a conference birthed out of her heart for teenage girls and mentorship across generations. Bethany currently resides in Altoona, Pennsylvania, with her husband, Micah and their bouncy boxer dog, Timber. Bethany is also the author of a children's book *Pickles and Prayer*. She enjoys drinking good coffee, shopping for good deals, and since she was a little girl, Bethany has always loved eating fruits and vegetables!

ABOUT SARAH VOGEL

Sarah Vogel is a self-taught artist, entrepreneur, and owner of The Clay Cup in Altoona, Pennsylvania. Sarah and her husband, Jeremy, are foodies at heart and enjoy cooking and exploring new foods together. They especially love spending time with their son, Judah, who brings so much joy to their lives. Sarah is the illustrator of the children's book *Pickles and Prayer*. Sarah also creates fun and trendy Polymer Clay Earrings, which she sells in her Etsy Shop. She primarily works in mediums such as watercolor, colored pencil, and ink. Her favorite subject to paint is food- because everyone can relate to that!

Other Books by Bethany Marshall

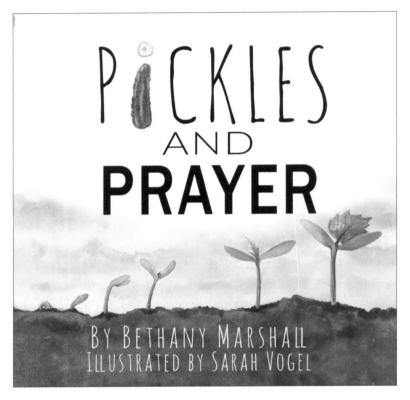

What could be more important than your child learning and discovering the power of prayer?

Pickles and Prayer has lively illustrations that draw the attention of young readers. The colorful pages and poetic text will help your child understand that prayer is simple, but it is also powerful. *Pickles and Prayer* also includes a homemade pickle recipe for the whole family to enjoy!

Also Available in Spanish!

PEPINILLOS Y **REZOS**

Por Bethany Marshall
Ilustrado por Sarah Vogel

CPSIA information can be obtained
at www.ICGtesting.com
Printed in the USA
BVHW022027270321
603293BV00001B/1